MW00637336

MYTHOLOGY

TIMELESS TALES OF GODS AND HEROES

by
Edith Hamilton

Teacher Guide

Written by
Gloria Levine, M.A.

Note

The text used to prepare this guide was the Penguin Group/Mentor softcover, ©1940, 1942 by Edith Hamilton, © renewed 1969 by Doris Fielding Reid. If other editions are used, page numbers may vary slightly.

Please note: Please assess the appropriateness of this book for the age level and maturity of your students prior to reading and discussing it with your class.

To order, contact your local school supply store, or—

Child Graphics Company, LLC
PO Box 5612
Hilton Head, SC 29938-5612
800.543.4880 • FAX 843.671.4665
www.childgraphics.com

Table of Contents

About the Author

Born in Germany and raised in the United States, Edith Hamilton (1867-1963) was a celebrated classicist and teacher. In this volume, she retells the great stories from Greek mythology (as well as Roman and Norse myths) that are the foundation for much of the literature we know today. She draws from tales written by ancient Greek writers over 2,000 years ago—Herodotus, Hesiod, Pindar, Homer, Lucian, Aeschylus, and others who actually believed in what they wrote.

These stories reflect a great deal of what the early Greeks, our intellectual forebears, were like. In them we see their worship of gods made in their own image, their celebration of human beings, their love of rationality, their explanations of the natural world. From Greek myths, we get an idea of what the Greeks believed and what they valued. These myths live on in our literature and art today. Knowing and thinking about them is important to our understanding of the rich cultural heritage we have acquired from ancient Greece.

While the Edith Hamilton collection was used in developing this guide, the suggested activities can also be used in classrooms where Bulfinch or other anthologies are used. Note that Hamilton uses mostly the Greek names and that Norse mythology, included in Part Seven of Hamilton, is not covered in this guide.

Initiating Activities

1. Discussion/Writing

Although many of the Greek myths have been around for over 2,000 years, the themes they address are still central to our lives today: love, hatred, anger, grief, jealousy, betrayal, fate, obedience, piety, death, war, friendship, happiness, and loyalty.

Pre-reading discussion and/or writing on these topics can provide a springboard for later discussion of myths' relevance to our contemporary world.

- *Love and Hatred:* Why does one person fall in love with another person? What qualities will the person you fall in love with probably have? Can you love and hate the same person? What situations arouse hatred?
- *Anger:* When is anger "unhealthy"? At what times is anger adaptive—"good"? What sorts of things make you angry? How do you cope with your anger?
- *Grief:* What sorts of losses arouse grief? What loss would you grieve most? How do people express their grief? How do people cope with grief?
- *Jealousy:* What situations arouse jealousy? Is jealousy a necessary part of love? Are women more jealous than men? Do men and women get jealous about the same things? How can you cope with your own jealousy and that of others? When does jealousy become "unhealthy"?

- *Betrayal:* How would you define betrayal? What are some famous instances of betrayal? How and why do some parents betray their children and vice versa? Have you ever experienced betrayal? How does it make you feel? What reactions does betrayal evoke?
- *Power/Hunger:* Why do some people seek power while others avoid it? Who are some people—historical and people known to you—who seem to enjoy wielding power? When do you feel the most powerful? How can the desire for power lead to good things? How can it lead to problems?
- *Sacrifice:* Do you believe that the "good of the many" should always be considered first? Do you think a political leader owes more to his or her country than to his or her children? Can you think of people who have "sacrificed" themselves to a cause? Would you risk your own life to save someone else's? Would you endanger the lives of your children to save others?
- *Fate:* Do you believe in "fate"? How much of your life do you have control over? When should you accept the way things are and when should you fight?
- *Obedience:* Whom should you obey? When should you obey and when should you question? Is there a difference between men and women in willingness to obey? To whom do you feel loyal? How do you show your sense of loyalty?
- *Death/War:* What do our present-day death rituals reveal about the way we view death? How is death depicted in the media today? Is killing ever justified? How do wars start? Who starts them?
- *Friendship:* What qualities do you look for in a friend? How do you show yourself to be a "good friend"? How important is friendship? What are you willing to sacrifice for friendship?
- *Happiness:* How would you define happiness? When are you happiest? Why do some people seem generally happier than others? What are some common situations that make people unhappy? How important is it to be happy?

2. Background on Greek Mythology

Have students view the film, "Those Fabulous Folks on Mount Olympus." (color; 30 minutes; $30 from Teacher's Discovery)

3. Reading to Younger Students

Have students either read selected myths to younger classes or prepare "stories on tape" for younger students. One excellent, beautifully illustrated version readers might use is: *Greek Gods and Heroes* by Alice Low, illustrated by Arvis Stewart. Another nice one is D'Aulaire's *Book of Greek Myths.*

4. Journal Writing

Before students read particular myths, have them freewrite in their journals using sentence starters like those on the next page. (The names of mythological characters and stories to which the sentence starters are particularly applicable precede each suggestion.)

(Prometheus)	Rebelling against injustice…
(Pandora)	My curiosity got me into trouble one time…
(Narcissus)	When a handsome guy is stuck up…
(Pyramus and Thisbe)	When parents try to keep young lovers apart…
(Daedalus)	When children ignore their parents' orders…
(Hercules)	A hero of mine who has been put to the test many times…
(Atalanta)	Today, an active and daring woman…
(Trojan War)	A desire for revenge can lead to war…
(Scylla and Charybdis)	The worst dilemma I ever faced…
(Cupid and Psyche)	When you break a promise…

5. Field Trip

If possible, arrange a visit to an art museum that contains paintings and sculptures based on Greek mythology. Or take an "electronic field trip" on the Internet, where you'll find a wealth of mythology images. Three wonderful sites are **PERSEUS at Tufts, The Louvre,** and **The Smithsonian On-Line.**

Another site with lots of examples from ancient sources and from later representations in art can be clicked on at—
http://web.UVic.CA/athena/bowman/myth/gods.html

For another site with several pieces of contemporary artwork, try
http://www.parnasse.com/erlist.htm

6. Anticipation Guide

Have students discuss the following statements. Return to these statements after students have read selected myths and have them discuss how the ideas in the myth apply to the statements.

There is a scientific explanation for everything.
Men and women are equally jealous.
An eye for an eye and a tooth for a tooth.
Some people really can predict the future.
Love conquers all.
In the end, people usually get their "just desserts."
Drinking usually leads to trouble.
Might makes right.
Most sons are inferior to their fathers.
You can't convince someone to love you.
Don't try to tamper with fate.
Don't get a swelled head.
Love 'em and leave 'em.
Live for today; you never know what tomorrow will bring.
Avoid extremes.
Be careful what you wish for; you might get it.
Accept what you can't change.
Reach for the stars.

Vocabulary Activities

1. Have students research various phrases that are derived from myth. For an ongoing whole-class activity, you might create a chart on posterboard or a transparency for the overhead, then add to the chart as you study the relevant myths.

Phrase/Word	What it means	Mythological source

Suggested phrases and words for research: Achilles' heel, titanic, saturnalia, "a young Adonis," phaethon, hydra, zephyr, ambrosia, panpipe, lethargic, boreal, cereal, morpheus, halcyon days, under the aegis, tantalize, arachnid, protean, Nike, chimera, python, "morphing," herculean, atlas, aurora, nemesis, dionysian, harpies, narcissism, Oedipal complex, Olympian, Trojan Horse, muse, calliope, siren song, golden fleece, argonaut, amazonian, Gordian knot, "Cassandra," mercurial, labyrinth, Pandora's box, promethean, Augean, procrustean bed, Midas touch, odyssey, voluptuous.

2. Have students research the figures after whom various places are named: the planets, the days of the week, the constellations, Europe, the Ionian Sea, the Aegean Sea, the Bosphorus, astrological signs.

3. Have students list as many words as they can find that are derived from a particular name from Greek myth, for example—

Cronos = chronic, chronology, chronometer, chronicler
Cyclops = cyclops, Cyclopie, cyclopia, bicycle
Jove = jovial, joviality
Muse = musician, musical, muse
Arachne = arachnid, arachnoid, araneiform
Pomona = pomme, pomology

4. Have students make a chart showing Greek and Latin names for each god and goddess on Mount Olympus. Have them find as many words and names as they can that are derived from these Greek and Latin ones.

Discussion Questions • Writing Ideas • Activities

PART ONE: THE GODS, THE CREATION, AND THE EARLIEST HEROES

1. The Gods

Synopsis: Cronus ruled the other enormous Titans until his son Zeus seized the throne. Zeus became the supreme ruler of twelve other gods, who succeeded the Titans: Poseidon (ruler of the sea), Hades (king of the dead), Hestia, Hera, Ares, Athena (daughter of Zeus, embodiment of wisdom), Apollo (master musician and archer), Aphrodite (goddess of love and beauty), Hermes (Zeus' swift messenger), Artemis (huntress, lady of wild things) and Hephaestus (lame God of fire, patron of handicrafts).

Discussion/Writing Questions

1. Who were the Titans and who was their leader? *(The Titans or "Elder Gods" were giants—offspring of Heaven and Earth—led by Cronus.)*

2. What 12 great Olympian gods succeeded the Titans? *(Zeus, Poseidon, Hades, Hestia, Hera, Ares, Athena, Apollo, Aphrodite, Hermes, Artemis, Hephaestus)* What do qualities of each show you about Greek attitudes? For example, what attitude toward creativity and disability is shown through the god, Hephaestus? *(Disability does not preclude creativity.)*

3. How did Zeus become ruler of the gods? *(He rebelled against his father, Cronus.)* Do you think he was a good leader? Why do you suppose Athena was his favorite daughter? What does he seem to value?

4. Who were some of the lesser gods of Olympus? *(Eros, Anteros, Himeros, Hymen, Hebe, Iris)* Which is your favorite? Which would you say is best known?

5. Who were the Muses and Graces? *(They were two bands of lovely sisters—the nine muses, daughters of Zeus and Mnemosyne, were each in charge of one of the arts; the three graces, daughters of Zeus and Eurynome, were the incarnation of grace and beauty.)* What does the verb "muse" mean? *(contemplate)* the noun? *(inspiration, guiding force)* What is "grace"? *(charm, elegance)* Do we value it much anymore?

6. How much support do you think we should give the arts? How can you give your personal support to the arts?

7. Who were the "Fates"? *(three creatures who gave to men at birth both evil and good and determined how long they would live)* Do you believe in "fate"?

8. You are one of the 11 gods or goddesses on Mt. Olympus other than Zeus. Give a campaign speech about why you, not Zeus, deserve to be leader of the gods.

2. The Two Great Gods of Earth

Of the gods, only two were truly mankind's friends—Demeter and Dionysus.

Synopsis: (a) **Demeter,** Goddess of the Corn, was grief-stricken when her daughter Persephone was taken by the God of the Underworld. Zeus freed Persephone, but her husband tricked her into eating a pomegranate seed, and she was forced to spend four months of the year in the world of the dead. During this sorrowful time, Demeter made the earth wintry and leafless.

Discussion/Writing Questions

1. How and why was Persephone taken from her mother? *(When she strayed from her companions to admire a narcissus, the Lord of the Underworld grabbed her and took her to Hades to be his bride. Zeus sent word that she could return to her mother, Demeter. Persephone had to return to Hades four months of the year because she ate a pomegranate seed.)* What real-world occurrence is explained by the myth of Persephone? *(the winter season)*

2. Was Demeter a good mother? *(She was very devoted and refused to let the earth bear fruit until she had her daughter back.)*

3. What Greek view of male/female relations is revealed by this story? *(Women have power derived from fertility.)*

4. Write another myth that explains the changing of seasons.

Synopsis: (b) Zeus' son, **Dionysus**—God of Wine—could be kind or cruel. He rescued his mother, a mortal, from the underworld and took her to live on Mt. Olympus. But his cruel side surfaced when he went to Thebes accompanied by the Maenads, women frenzied with wine. When Pentheus imprisoned him, the mad women—including Pentheus' own mother and sisters made crazy by Dionysus—tore Pentheus limb from limb.

Discussion/Writing Questions

1. How did Pentheus die? *(Crazed women, including followers of Dionysus and Pentheus' family, tore him apart after he imprisoned Dionysus.)*

2. Do you think Dionysus was responsible for Pentheus' death?

3. What view of alcohol do you think is presented by this story?

4. What do you think about advertising alcoholic beverages on television? Does it encourage irresponsible behavior, especially among underage drinkers?

3. How the World and Mankind Were Created

Synopsis: Love was born from darkness and created Light; the creation of Earth was next and the first living creatures—children of Mother Earth and Father Heaven—were gigantic monsters (Titans, Cyclops, fifty-headed monsters, Giants, and Furies). One Titan, Cronus, became lord of the universe for ages; then one of his sons, Zeus, became ruler of heaven and earth. One Titan, Prometheus, sided with Zeus. Humans were created (by Prometheus and his brother Epimetheus or by the gods, depending on which story you read). Prometheus stole fire for man and was punished by Zeus, who had him chained to a rock, where eagles pecked at his liver. In another account of the creation, Zeus sent a flood to destroy wicked mankind but Deucalion and Pyrrha survived in a wooden chest and Zeus took pity on them. The stones they cast upon the earth became humans.

Discussion/Writing Questions

1. What is the "theogony"? *(the account of the origin of the gods)*

2. How were heaven and earth formed? *(Mother Earth was created out of chaos and many years later bore Ouranos, Father Heaven.)* Who were their children? *(Titans, Cyclops, Giants, Furies)* Who were their grandchildren? *(gods)*

   Draw a family tree that shows the relationship of Ouranos and Gaea to the 12 gods and goddesses of Mt. Olympus.

3. Why was Prometheus punished? *(He helped Zeus fight Cronus and the other Titans, but stole fire and gave it to man. Zeus thought he loved men too well.)*

4. Do you think Prometheus is someone to admire? Have you ever been in a situation like his?

5. The gods were a "family" with Zeus as the father-figure. How did this group make decisions? How is this like/different from the way decisions are made in your family?

6. How were Deucalion and Pyrrha like the biblical Noah and his wife? *(Pyrrha and her husband Deucalion were survivors of the great flood.)*

7. You are Zeus. Design Mother's and Father's Day cards for your parents.

8. Write about a time when you, like Prometheus, risked something to stand up for what you believed in.

4. The Earliest Heroes

Synopsis: (a) **Prometheus and Io**—Zeus fell in love with a princess, Io. He turned her into a white heifer to try to trick his jealous wife, Hera. Hera drove Io from her home and sent a gad-fly to plague her. Chained to his rock, Prometheus tried to comfort Io with predictions of a happier future for her.

Discussion/Writing Questions

1. How and why was Io punished? *(Io was turned into a cow by Zeus; she was then plagued by a fly sent by Hera who was jealous of Zeus' attentions to the maiden.)*

2. How did Prometheus try to comfort Io? *(He told her that in the distant future she would reach the Nile, be restored to human form, and be happy again.)* What else could he have said?

Synopsis: (b) **Europa**—Zeus also fell in love with Europa and changed himself into a bull. Unsuspecting, she jumped on his back and found herself crossing the sea accompanied by strange sea-gods. Zeus took her to the island of Crete where she bore him several sons—including Minos and Rhadamanthus.

Discussion/Writing Questions

1. Why did Zeus change himself into a bull? *(He wanted to entice the maiden Europa while in disguise, in case Hera should show up.)*

2. Why do you suppose Europe was named after this particular woman? What other myth-derived name would you have suggested?

3. Write a conversation that Io and Europa have about Zeus.

Synopsis: (c) **The Cyclops Polyphemus**—On their way home after the destruction of Troy, Odysseus and his men stopped at an island and entered the cave of a one-eyed monster, Polyphemus. After the monster had killed several of the men, Odysseus and the others escaped by blinding him and hiding under his rams as they left the cave.

Discussion/Writing Questions

1. Why did Odysseus blind Polyphemus? *(The Cyclops had already killed several of his men and would devour the rest unless they could escape from the cave.)*

2. Do you have any sympathy for Polyphemus?

3. Write a poem about Polyphemus. This might be a limerick Odysseus makes up, a bitterness poem from Polyphemus' point of view, a revenge poem, etc.

5. Flower Myths

Synopsis: Narcissus—Jealous Hera silenced the pretty nymph, Echo, taking away her power ever to speak first. When Echo tried to get the attention of handsome, cruel Narcissus, she could only echo him. She was unable to help him when he fell in love with his own reflection in a pool; he pined away while staring at it. A flower bloomed where his body had lain.

Discussion/Writing Questions

1. How and why was Echo punished? *(Hera suspected that Zeus was in love with Echo and punished the nymph by removing her power of speech—except repetition of what had just been said to her.)*

2. Do you think Narcissus deserved to have a flower named after him? *(Narcissus was a handsome young man who fell in love with his own reflection and died rather than tear himself away to get food; a flower bloomed where his body had lain.)*

3. What does this story show about qualities the Greeks did/didn't value? *(They valued free speech, thought it unwise to be too vain and self-absorbed.)*

Synopsis: Hyacinth—The god Apollo threw a discus and accidentally killed his friend Hyacinthus; a flower grew where his blood fell, mingling with Apollo's tears.

Discussion/Writing Question

Compare and contrast Hyacinthus and Narcissus. (*A flower grew up where each young man died; Hyacinthus died when the discus thrown by his friend Apollo struck him in the head; Narcissus pined away.*)

Synopsis: Adonis—A crimson flower, the anemone, sprang up where the blood of Adonis, the young man loved by both Aphrodite and Persephone, fell when he was gored by a boar.

Discussion/Writing Questions

1. How did the anemone flower supposedly come into being? (*It grew where the body of Adonis had lain.*)

2. What does the expression "a young Adonis" mean? (*handsome young man*)

3. Does this story remind you of any poems or fairy tales you have read?

4. Create a poster or collage about these three types of flowers that captures your impressions of the stories about their origins: narcissus, hyacinth, anemone.

PART TWO: STORIES OF LOVE AND ADVENTURE

6. Cupid and Psyche

Synopsis: Cupid, son of jealous Venus, fell in love with the beautiful Psyche. The oracle of Apollo advised her parents to leave her on a hill to be claimed by her future husband, a fearful serpent. She was rescued by Zephyr and delivered to Cupid, who she could hear but not see. She felt that her unseen husband was no monster, but she promised that she would never try to see him. Swayed by her jealous, wicked sisters, she broke her promise and looked at her husband, accidentally burning him with lamp oil. He fled, and when she sought Venus' help, she was given several trials which she passed with the help of some ants, a reed, an eagle, and a tower. Psyche was made immortal, Cupid forgave her, and all ended happily.

Discussion/Writing Questions

1. What promise did Psyche break and what were the consequences? (*She broke her promise not to look at her husband.*) Who helped Psyche? (*ants, a reed, an eagle, a tower*)

2. Where else have you seen this idea of forbidding a woman to look at her husband?

3. What associations do you have with the words "Cupid" and "Psyche"? How are these terms related? (*Cupid = heart/love; Psyche = ego/mind/soul. We think of our heart as governing our feelings and our head as in charge of our thoughts and decisions.*)

4. Would you want to be immortal?

5. Write an interior monologue showing Psyche's thoughts as her husband flees from her sight.

7. Eight Brief Tales of Lovers

Synopsis: (a) **Pyramus and Thisbe**—These were young lovers whose parents tried to keep them apart. When Pyramus arrived under the white mulberry tree, where he was supposed to meet Thisbe, he saw a lioness there who had made a recent kill. Thinking his beloved Thisbe was dead, Pyramus stabbed himself. Thisbe found the dying Pyramus under the tree, whose fruit was now red, and killed herself.

Discussion/Writing Questions

1. Who kept Pyramus and Thisbe apart? *(their parents)* Why do you suppose they were against Pyramus and Thisbe's marrying?

2. What natural phenomenon does this story explain? *(why the mulberry changes from white to red)*

3. How is this like the story of Romeo and Juliet? *(Both are about young lovers who commit suicide when their families try to keep them apart.)*

4. Into what comedy does Shakespeare incorporate the story of Pyramus and Thisbe? *(A Midsummer Night's Dream)*

5. Do you find Pyramus and Thisbe admirable or silly?

6. What do you think your friends might be trying to tell you if they sent you a branch from a mulberry tree as a gift?

7. Write a short script for a play production of "Pyramus and Thisbe."

Synopsis: (b) **Orpheus and Eurydice**—When Eurydice was killed by a snake and died, her husband Orpheus—a wonderful musician—tried to rescue his wife from the underworld. He failed at the last minute by disobeying Hades' instructions not to look back at her. He wandered the land sadly playing his lyre and was finally killed by a band of Maenads.

Discussion/Writing Questions

1. Why did Orpheus fail to bring his wife back from Hades? *(He looked back at her at the last minute, thinking they were at last free of the underworld.)*

2. How was Orpheus like Psyche? *(She too failed by looking at her husband.)*

3. Can you think of other stories, old or new, where someone tried to bring a loved one back from the dead?

4. You are Orpheus. Write the words to a memorial song you might sing about Eurydice.

Synopsis: (c) Ceyx and Alcyone—When Ceyx the king was drowned in a shipwreck, his devoted wife, Alcyone, saw his dead body in a dream and went to the shore the next day. The gods took pity on the couple, changing both Ceyx and Alcyone into seabirds and reuniting them forever. Every year there are seven days of tranquility when Alcyon broods over her nest—"Alcyon" or "Halcyon" days.

Discussion/Writing Questions

1. Why were Ceyx and Alcyone turned into birds? *(The gods felt sorry for the couple after the king drowned in a shipwreck, so husband and wife were reunited as birds.)*

2. What are "halcyon days"? *(happy, carefree times)* Find out what sort of medication "Halcyon" is. Find a line of poetry that refers to "halcyon days."

3. Write a description of certain halcyon days you have known.

Synopsis: (d) Pygmalion and Galatea—When Pygmalion, a sculptor, fell in love with his statue, Galatea, Venus heard his prayer and brought the statue to life.

Discussion/Writing Questions

1. Why did Pygmalion fall in love with a statue and not a real woman? *(He didn't like women, but found that he had fashioned a perfect woman from stone.)*

2. Who brought the statue to life? *(Venus)* Do you think Pygmalion was as happy with the real woman as he had been with the statue?

3. Why do you think George Bernard Shaw titled his play "Pygmalion"? How are the main characters of "My Fair Lady," the film/musical adaptation of the story, like Pygmalion and Galatea? *(An intellectual man tries to "mold" a lower class woman by teaching her diction and etiquette and finds that she has a will and feelings of her own.)*

4. Rewrite the story of Pygmalion and Galatea set somewhere in the here and now.

Synopsis: (e) Baucis and Philemon—Jupiter (Zeus) and Mercury (Ares) went down to Earth disguised as mortals. Spurned by most people, they were treated hospitably by a poor old couple, Baucis and Philemon. As a reward, the couple were made priests of a grand temple and their wish to die together was granted. In the end, they turned into an oak and linden tree growing from a single trunk.

Discussion/Writing Questions

1. How and why were Baucis and Philemon rewarded? *(They were kind to the disguised Zeus and Ares and were rewarded by being made priests—and, at death, by being turned into an oak/linden tree.)*

2. Where have you seen this idea—"great" individuals disguised as "everyday people"—before?

3. What does this story show about the Greeks' attitude toward trees and other plant life? *(Plant life was held in reverence.)*

4. Write a short essay with this topic sentence: "Character is what you do when you don't realize anyone is watching." Include supportive evidence from this myth and from your own experience.

Synopsis: (f) Endymion—This beautiful youth was put into an eternal sleep by the Moon, who visits him each night and covers him with kisses.

Discussion/Writing Questions

1. Why doesn't Endymion ever waken? *(The Moon has made him sleep forever so that she can visit him each night.)*

2. Is the Moon happy? *(She sighs mournfully.)* Do you think she really loves Endymion? Wouldn't she have pity on him and let him waken if she did?

3. Is this like what sometimes happens in real life when a person wants someone he or she "cannot have"?

4. How is this like other stories of "unrequited love"? How is it different?

5. You are the Moon. Write a note of apology to Endymion.

Synopsis: (g) Daphne—Daphne was a huntress who fled Apollo when he declared his love. When she begged her father, the river-god Peneus for help, he turned her into a laurel tree. Apollo declared that her leaves would always crown his victors.

Discussion/Writing Questions

1. Why was Daphne turned into a tree? *(Her father turned her into a tree to help her escape from Apollo.)* Why do you suppose she and her father didn't just tell Apollo to take a hike?

2. Why did Daphne flee? *(She didn't want to be taken by Apollo, probably because maidens pursued by gods often ended up having to kill their children or getting killed, themselves.)* Why do you think Apollo still wanted Daphne even when it became obvious she didn't want to be with him? Is that the way people act in real life?

3. According to this myth, why are Greek victors often shown with laurel crowns? *(When Apollo saw Daphne change into a laurel tree, he declared that victors should always wear laurel crowns.)*

Synopsis: (h) Alpheus and Arethusa—Arethusa was another huntress who wanted nothing to do with men. When the god of the river, Alpheus, declared his love, she tried to flee. When she called to her goddess, Artemis, for help, she was changed into a sacred spring.

Discussion/Writing Questions

1. How was Arethusa like Daphne? *(Both loved hunting; neither wanted to go the love-and-marriage route.)*

2. How did Arethusa turn into a spring? *(To help her escape, Artemis turned her into a spring and made an underground tunnel from Greece to Sicily for Arethusa to flow through.)* Given a choice, do you think Arethusa would have agreed to this?

3. Why do you think there are so many myths about women who wanted nothing to do with men? What was the role of women in Greek society at this time?

4. Write the conversation Daphne's father has with Artemis.

8. The Quest of the Golden Fleece

Synopsis: When Jason, son of a King, came to claim his right to the throne, King Pelias sent him to Colchis to recover the golden fleece hoping Jason would never return. Jason had a ship called the Argo built and set off on his quest with fifty volunteers. Jason and the Argonauts faced many dangers. They saved the starving Phineus by chasing off the Harpies who always snatched his food, and in return he advised them how to get through the Clashing Rocks. When they arrived in Colchis, the king asked the brave Argonauts to perform an impossible task before handing over the golden fleece: plow a field with fire-breathing bulls and plant the teeth of a dragon that would become an army they must destroy. Little did the king know that his daughter, Medea—a witch—would fall in love with Jason and use her magic to help him. The Argonauts set sail for home with the golden fleece and faced several more dangers on the way including Scylla and Charybdis, two monsters on either side of a passage that devoured passing ships, and a rock-throwing giant. Jason returned to find that the king had killed his father, causing his mother's suicide. In revenge, Jason had Pelias cut up and boiled by his own daughters. Jason fell in love with another woman and the vengeful Medea killed her, then killed her own children fathered by Jason.

Discussion/Writing Questions

1. Who sent Jason on a dangerous quest? Why? *(King Pelias wanted to get rid of Jason, the rightful heir to the throne, and sent him for the golden fleece.)*

2. Why do you think this story is one of the most famous of the myths?

3. Why were prospectors during the California goldrush known as "argonauts"? *(Like the mythical men, they were on a quest for gold.)*

4. How did Medea help Jason? Why? *(When Cupid made Medea fall in love with Jason, Medea gave Jason ointment to keep him and his weapons invincible; she told him to throw a stone among the dragon-teeth men; she lulled the serpent guarding the fleece to sleep with a song while Jason grabbed the prize; when her brother pursued, she killed him; she prayed to the hounds of Hades to destroy the bronze man on Crete; she helped bring about the death of Pelias.)* How do you think Medea felt about betraying her father? Have you ever felt torn between loyalty to parents and to others?

5. How did Medea get revenge after Jason deserted her? *(She killed Jason's bride and her own children fathered by Jason.)* How did Medea justify killing her children? *(She didn't want them to live to be ill-used by strangers.)* Do you feel at all sorry for her? Was Jason to blame? Do you think Medea was evil?

6. Do you think Pelias deserved to die the way he did?

7. Write three descriptions of Jason from the points of view of different people who knew him.

9. Four Great Adventures

Synopsis: (a) **Phaethon**—Phaethon, the son of Apollo the sun god, drove his father's chariot through the skies. Elated, he failed to heed his father's advice and lost control of the chariot. Zeus hit the chariot with a thunderbolt to keep the world from being destroyed and Phaethon was killed.

Discussion/Writing Questions

1. Why did Zeus kill Phaethon? *(Otherwise Phaethon's chariot might have destroyed the world.)*

2. Who was most to blame for Phaethon's death; the boy—for failing to heed his father's advice? the father—for allowing his son to take the chariot? Zeus—for hitting the chariot with a thunderbolt?

3. Zeus apparently reasoned that "the good of the many" has priority over what is "good for one." If one innocent person's death will save the lives of others, do you feel that person should die? Where have you seen this idea come up in other stories, songs, poems, movies?

4. Suppose you are reading a Thomas Hardy novel in which a "phaeton" appears. What is a phaeton? *(type of carriage)*

5. You are an officer investigating the death of Phaethon. Write up the notes of your interview with Zeus and Phaethon's father.

Synopsis: (b) **Pegasus and Bellerophon**—Brave young Bellerophon rode Pegasus, the wild winged horse, and slew the Chimaera, a fire-breathing monster. When he began to think "thoughts too great for man," he lost Pegasus to Zeus.

Discussion/Writing Questions

1. Imagine a picture of Pegasus, Bellerophon, and the Chimaera. What do you see?

2. Who was Bellerophon's father? *(Glaucus)* Why did the gods kill him? *(He dared feed his horses on human flesh to make them mightier.)*

3. How did Bellerophon get the horse he wanted? *(Athena helped him get Pegasus.)*

4. Why did Proetus send Bellerophon on a dangerous quest? *(Rebuffed by the young man, Proetus' angry wife told her husband that Bellerophon had wronged her.)*

5. How did Bellerophon slay the Chimaera? *(He avoided her flames by soaring over her on Pegasus while shooting arrows at her.)* When we speak of a "chimera" today, what do we mean? *(a horrible creature of the imagination)*

6. How did Bellerophon die? *(The gods punished him for trying to ride to Olympus by having Pegasus throw him; he wandered alone until he died.)*

7. What happened to Pegasus? *(He went to Olympus; whenever Zeus wanted thunder and lightning, Pegasus brought it to him.)*

8. What does this story show about Greek values and beliefs? For instance, what did the Greeks think of ambitious men who thought they were as good as the gods? What did they apparently think of human sacrifice?

9. You are a news reporter. Write an eyewitness account of the slaying of the Chimaera.

Synopsis: (c) **Otus and Ephialtes**—These twin brothers were arrogant giants fathered by Poseidon. They angered Zeus by chaining up the god Ares, threatening to climb to heaven, and planning to abduct Artemis. She turned herself into a hind (deer) and when the brothers each hurled their spears at her, they killed each other.

Discussion/Writing Questions

1. How did these twins die? *(They accidentally killed each other while chasing a "deer"—actually Artemis.)* Did they get their just deserts?

2. What do you notice about many of the twins in Greek mythology? *(They are often at each other's throats.)*

3. What does this story show you is one sure way of angering the gods? *(trying to prove you are superior to them)*

4. Write an obituary for the twins.

Synopsis: (d) **Daedalus**—Daedalus, an architect and inventor, fathered Icarus. After being imprisoned by King Minos in the Labyrinth, they constructed two pairs of wings and prepared to make their escape. Unfortunately, once in the air, Icarus grew giddy and ignored his father's advice. When he flew too close to the sun, the wax in his wings melted and he plunged into the sea.

Discussion/Writing Questions

1. Why were Daedalus and Icarus imprisoned? *(King Minos realized that Daedalus had helped Theseus escape from the Labyrinth.)* How did they escape? *(They made two pairs of wings.)*

2. How was Icarus like Phaethon? *(When both took flight, they lost control.)*

3. Why did Daedalus ignore his father's advice? *(Delighted, he lost his head.)* Have you ever been in a similar situation?

4. Do you think the Greeks told this story to their children to remind them to listen to their parents?

5. Read the poem "Musée des Beaux Arts" by W. H. Auden, which contains a reference to the fall of Icarus.

6. View a print of the famous painting by Brueghel, mentioned in Auden's poem, "Landscape with the Fall of Icarus" (on display at the Museum of Fine Arts in Brussels).

17

7. View the award-winning film based on the Daedalus myth, "Sun Flight." Discuss Gerald McDermott's use of changing colors to illustrate different portions of the ill-fated flight.

8. Write a prayer poem for Icarus from his father's point of view.

PART THREE: THE GREAT HEROES BEFORE THE TROJAN WAR

10. Perseus

Synopsis: Perseus, fathered by Zeus, slew Medusa with Hermes' help. Hermes gave Perseus an unbreakable sword and told him he had to obtain winged sandals, a magic wallet, and a cap to make him invisible. Perseus enlisted the help of the Gray women by snatching the eyeball shared by all three, then beheaded Medusa, put her head in the wallet and headed for home rescuing his future bride, Andromeda, from a sea monster on the way.

Discussion/Writing Questions

1. How and why did Acrisius put his daughter and grandson in danger? *(He had them put to sea because of a prophecy that his grandson would murder him.)*

2. How and why did Perseus slay Medusa? *(Perseus thought that he was getting a wedding gift for the King, who actually asked for the head so that he could get rid of Perseus and marry his mother, Danae; Hermes helped Perseus by equipping him with sandals, a magic wallet, a cap of invisibility, and a sword. Armed with a special shield by Athena, Perseus cut off Medusa's head.)*

3. Who was Andromeda? *(Perseus' future wife)* How did Perseus save her? *(He cut off the head of the great snake to which she was to be sacrificed.)*

4. Do you think there was a single good bone in Medusa's body? Do you sympathize with her?

5. Does the magic in this story remind you of that in any others? For example, where in Tolkien do you see an article that makes the bearer invisible?

6. Write down Medusa's final thoughts.

11. Theseus

Synopsis: Brave young Theseus killed the Minotaur (a creature, half bull and half man, who had been devouring young men and women as sacrificial offerings every nine years) with the help of the king's daughter, Ariadne. After using a ball of thread Ariadne had given him to find his way out of the Labyrinth, Theseus abandoned Ariadne and returned home. His father committed suicide, thinking that Theseus had been killed, and Theseus became King of Athens.

Discussion/Writing Questions

1. Who was Procrustes and what happened to him? *(He was a robber who stretched or amputated limbs of travelers to make them conform to the length of his bed, killed in a similar fashion by Theseus on his way to see his father.)* Today, what does "Procrustean" mean? *(tending to produce conformity by violent or arbitrary means)*

2. Who almost poisoned Theseus and why? *(King Aegeus, jealous about the young man's popularity, almost poisoned him then recognized him as his son.)*

3. Why did the people of Athens sacrifice seven young men and women each year? *(King Minos of Crete demanded this reparation after his son, a guest of King Aegeus, was killed by a bull.)*

4. How and why did Theseus kill the Minotaur? *(The Minotaur was devouring the young people of Athens, so Theseus went into the Labyrinth where he was kept and beat the creature to death.)* With whose help? *(King Minos' daughter gave Theseus a ball of string to find his way out of the Labyrinth.)*

5. What did Ariadne and Medea have in common? *(They were both abandoned by the men they had helped.)* Why do you suppose Theseus abandoned Ariadne?

6. How did Theseus' father die? *(He saw the black sail on his son's ship, mistakenly thought his son had died, and killed himself.)* Do you think Theseus should feel personally guilty about his father's death? In what other myths do we see suicide or thoughts of suicide? What did the Greek attitude toward taking one's own life seem to be?

7. You are Ariadne. Write an entry in your journal about your memories of meeting Theseus and the experience of knowing him. Include both "pluses" and "minuses."

12. Hercules

Synopsis: Hercules, son of Zeus and Alcmena, the strongest man in the world performed 12 great labors to cleanse himself of the terrible sins he had committed. (Hera, jealous of Alcmena, had caused Hercules to go mad and kill his own wife and children.) These labors were: killing the lion of Nemea; killing the many-headed Hydra; obtaining a white deer with golden horns; capturing the boar of Mount Erymanthus alive; cleaning King Augeas' yard of bull dung; ridding a marsh of Stymphalian birds with their dangerous beaks; catching the fearsome bull that lived on Crete; bringing back the man-eating mares of Thrace; obtaining the golden girdle of Hippolyte, queen of the Amazons; bringing back the cattle of terrible King Geryon; bringing back the golden apples of the Hesperides; capturing Cerberus, the three-headed dog of the underworld.

Discussion/Writing Questions

1. How did Hercules show his "specialness" at an early age? *(As a baby, he killed two snakes that had entered the crib he shared with his brother.)* Was he very bright? *(No, he did many rather silly things.)*

2. What were the 12 labors and why did Hercules perform them? *(To make up for killing his wife and children after Hera made him go mad, he killed the lion of Nemea; killed the many-headed Hydra; obtained a white deer with golden horns; captured the boar of Mount Erymanthus alive; cleaned King Augeas' yard of bull dung; ridded a marsh of Stymphalian birds with their dangerous beaks; caught the fearsome bull that lived on Crete; brought back the man-eating mares of Thrace; obtained the golden girdle of Hippolyte, queen of the Amazons; brought back the cattle of terrible King Geryon; brought back the golden apples of the Hesperides; and captured Cerberus, the three-headed dog of the underworld.)* Which do you think was the hardest of the labors? What mnemonic device could you use to remember these? Where does the term "mnemonic" come from?

3. How would you describe Hercules' personality? What would you change to make him the "perfect hero"?

4. How did Hercules die? *(Jealous Deianira sent him a robe that tortured him until he killed himself.)* Does the robe he wore to his death remind you of another mythical robe? *(the one Medea sent Jason's bride)*

5. What do you think of the TV show, "Hercules: The Legendary Journeys"? How much Greek myth do you find incorporated into the program?

6. Why do you think Hercules is one of the most well-known and well-liked of the Greek heroes? How does he compare with current superheroes like Superman or the X-Men?

7. List 12 labors you would give Hercules today.

13. Atalanta

Synopsis: Atalanta, an active and spirited princess who preferred the idea of hunting to marriage, agreed to marry any suitor who could beat her in a footrace; losers would die. Hippomenes won the race by distracting her with some golden apples.

Discussion/Writing Questions
1. Who raised Atalanta? *(a bear)*

2. How did the hunt for the Calydonian boar end? *(Atalanta wounded the boar; Meleaguer finished it off and gave her the skin. When his uncles protested he killed them, and later his mother caused Meleaguer's death.)*

3. Why did Atalanta race her suitors? *(She didn't want to marry, and thought she could dispose of her suitors by agreeing to marry the one who could beat her in a race—something she thought nobody could do.)*

4. Why do you suppose Atalanta required losers to die? Why do you suppose these men would willingly risk death to marry Atalanta, someone they didn't know?

5. How did Hippomenes win Atalanta? *(He beat her in a race by distracting her with golden apples.)* Do you think she loved him? What happened to them both in the end? *(They were turned into lions when they angered Zeus or Aphrodite.)*

6. Of what other mythical women does Atalanta remind you?

7. Do you think Atalanta is a good role model for little girls?

8. You are Atalanta. You have been asked to give a speech at a rally held by NOW (National Organization of Women). Write the speech.

PART FOUR: THE HEROES OF THE TROJAN WAR

14. The Trojan War

Synopsis: Zeus chose Paris to judge who was the fairest—Aphrodite, Athena, or Hera. He chose Aphrodite and she rewarded him by making the most beautiful woman in the world, Helen, wife of Menelaus, fall in love with Paris. Helen ran off with Paris and Menelaus gathered an army to sail to Troy and fight for her. The Greeks and Trojans fought for ten years outside the wall.

Discussion/Writing Questions

1. How did the Trojan war begin? *(Helen, the wife of a Greek named Menelaus, was taken off by a Trojan named Paris.)* Did any recent wars or conflicts start in a similar way?

2. Why did Helen go with Paris? *(She fell in love with him.)* Why did he want her? *(As a reward for selecting Aphrodite as the most beautiful of three goddesses, Paris was given the most beautiful woman, Helen.)*

3. How long did the two sides fight? *(The Trojan War lasted for ten years.)*

4. Briefly summarize the story of the Trojan War in an alphabet poem or story. The first line begins with a word starting with the letter, "A." The next line begins with a word starting with "B," and so on.

15. The Fall of Troy

Synopsis: Odysseus came up with an idea for tricking the Trojans. He directed the construction of a huge wooden horse. Part of the Greek army sailed away while another group of men hid themselves in the horse. Thinking the horse was an offering to Athena, and ignoring a seer's warning to beware the Greeks even when they bear gifts, the curious Trojans took the horse inside the gates. The Greeks sprang out, killing most of the Trojan leaders. The Greeks won the war and Helen was led back to her husband, Menelaus.

Discussion/Writing Questions

1. Who won the war? *(the Greeks)* How? *(They hid inside the Trojan horse and sprang out when the horse was taken inside the gates.)*

2. When you read a newspaper article that mentions a "Trojan Horse" what phrase could you mentally substitute? *(trick, diversion)*

3. Why did Achilles and Agamemnon quarrel and what was the outcome? *(The prophet Calchas declared that Agamemnon could save the Greek army from plague if he would only appease Apollo by giving up the woman, Chryseis, he had "won" as a war prize. Agamemnon finally did so, but then took Achilles' "prize," the girl Briseis. Angry, Achilles refused to help Agamemnon battle the Trojans.)*

4. Whose side was Zeus on? *(He favored the Trojans, but didn't want to openly oppose Hera, who favored the Greeks.)*

5. Why was Achilles so intent on killing Hector? *(Hector had killed Achilles' good friend, Patroclus.)* How did he dishonor Hector's body? *(by dragging it behind his chariot)* Why did he finally allow Hector's body to be buried? *(He took pity on Hector's father, Priam.)*

6. How do you think Menelaus and Helen felt about Helen's return after the war was over? Write two interior monologues, showing what each was thinking at the time of their reunion.

16. The Adventures of Odysseus

Synopsis: Because the gods were angry with the Greeks for failing to give thanks, many ships sank and Odysseus ended up wandering for ten years before coming home to his wife Penelope and son, Telemachus. Along the way, he blinded the cylops, Polyphemus; he was blown off course when his men opened a bag of storms given to them by King Aeolus; his men were changed into pigs by the sorceress, Circe; he visited the underworld; he had himself bound to the mast while the ship passed the enticing Sirens; some of his crew were killed by Scylla and Charybdis; most of his men were drowned for killing the cattle of Helios; Odysseus was virtually imprisoned by Calypso, who loved him. Finally, with the help of Ino, a sea nymph, Nausicaa, and her father, King Alcinous, Odysseus returned to Ithaca. His wife Penelope had held off her suitors by promising to marry one when her weaving was finished, but unraveled her work each night. Odysseus and Telemachus slew the suitors and Odysseus regained his throne, reunited with his wife after a twenty-year absence.

Discussion/Writing Questions

1. Why didn't Odysseus go right home after the war? *(Athena wanted the Greeks punished.)* Why were the gods angry? *(The Greeks hadn't given proper thanks to the gods; they had dared to lay violent hands on Priam's daughter while she was in Athena's temple.)* What does this show you about the Greek view of the gods? *(The gods demanded homage.)*

2. What were some of the dangers and problems faced by Odysseus? *(He blinded Polyphemus the Cyclops, was swept away by the tempest released when his men opened the bag from King Aeolus, escaped from Circe who changed his men to swine, passed the Island of the Sirens, passed through the passage of Scylla and Charybdis, escaped from the Island of the Sun where the rest of his crew were killed for slaying the sacred oxen.)*

3. Was Odysseus faithful to Penelope while he was away? *(He lived with Circe and Calypso, but missed Penelope.)* Was she true to him? *(yes, apparently)*

4. Why did Penelope do so much weaving? *(She put off the suitors by promising to accept one when she was finished with her weaving but each night she unraveled her work.)*

5. How did Odysseus regain his throne? *(He and his son Telemachus slew the suitors.)* How long had he been away? *(20 years)*

6. What do you find to be the most memorable part of this story? Which parts are most often popularized?

7. As you watch "Star Trek" and its various spin-offs, what do you notice about the incorporation of elements from myth? What themes are common to many myths and many "Star Trek" episodes?

8. Write Odysseus' curriculum vitae (résumé).

17. The Adventures of Aeneas

Synopsis: This Trojan hero, son of Venus, survived the fall of Troy and escaped with other Trojans to Italy, where he founded Rome. On his way, he and his company landed on the island of the Cyclopes, encountered the Harpies, and passed by the strait guarded by Scylla and Charybdis. Aeneas fell in love with Dido, who had founded Carthage, but he ultimately left her and she committed suicide. Aeneas descended to the underworld, where he met Dido. He arrived in Italy and a furious war raged. Aeneas married Lavinia and founded the Roman race.

Discussion/Writing Questions

1. Compare and contrast Aeneas and Odysseus. *(Aeneas—Trojan and Odysseus—Greek; both wandered for years after the Trojan War.)* Which do you admire more?

2. What city was founded by Dido? *(Carthage)* How did Aeneas treat Dido? *(He ultimately deserted her.)* Was her death his fault? *(She committed suicide, in sorrow.)*

3. What would you say Aeneas is best remembered for? *(founding Rome)*

4. You are Aeneas. You keep a ship's log that summarizes what happens on your journey. Write three entries.

18. The House of Atreus

Synopsis: (a) **Tantalus and Niobe**—Tantalus, mortal son of Zeus, was condemned to stand for all time in a pool unable to quench his thirst. His daughter Niobe, queen of Thebes, arrogantly defied Leto the Titan, who punished Niobe by having all fourteen of her children killed and by changing her into a stone.

Discussion/Writing Questions

1. How and why was Tantalus punished? *(He boiled his own son and tried to serve him up to the gods to trick them into cannibalism; they discovered his trickery and put him in a pool in Hades where he could not reach the water to drink, nor reach fruit trees to eat.)*

2. What does "tantalizing" mean? *(alluring, tempting)*

3. Who was Niobe and how was she punished? *(Tantalus' daughter was punished for saying she was better than the goddess, Leto; Apollo and Artemis struck down all of her children as punishment.)* Who were some other figures in mythology punished for excessive pride?

4. When does pride become excessive and when is it a good thing?

5. Tantalus and Niobe were both punished without having had a trial. Imagine that each had had a trial. Write the transcript of the statements each makes about his/her "crime" while under oath.

Synopsis: (b) **Agamemnon and His Children**—Agamemnon, commander of the Greek forces at Troy, returned safely home after the war only to be murdered by his wife's lover. His wife, Clytemnestra, was angry that Agamemnon had killed their daughter, Iphigenia, ten years before albeit unwillingly, as a sacrifice.

Discussion/Writing Questions

1. How did Agamemnon die? *(He was killed by his wife and her lover.)* Did he deserve what he got?

2. What role did Agamemnon play in his daughter's death? *(He told the men to lift his daughter over the altar, where she was killed in sacrifice.)* Do you blame him for what he did?

3. In what other stories have you seen the theme of human sacrifice played out? What did the Greeks seem to think of this practice?

4. Who was Cassandra? *(Priam's daughter, a prophetess—gift to Agamemnon, killed by Clytemnestra)* What do we mean when we call someone a "Cassandra" today? *(someone who prophesies doom and often, someone whom we don't believe but should)*

5. You are Clytemnestra. Write two entries in your journal; your thoughts the night after you kill your husband and the dream that you have that night.

Synopsis: (c) **Iphigenia among the Taurians**—In one version of the story of Iphigenia, she was spared from sacrifice by Artemis, who took her to the land of the fierce Taurians where she had the terrible job of overseeing human sacrifices. Her brother, Orestes, was brought before her for sacrifice with his friend Pylades, and she escaped with them both by ship, aided by Athena.

Discussion/Writing Questions

1. How did Iphigenia end up with the job of overseeing human sacrifices? *(In an alternate ending to the story, Iphigenia was saved from sacrifice by Artemis, who took her to the land of the Taurians where she was made priestess of the temple and given the awful task of conducting sacrifices.)* Did she have a choice? Do you blame her for accepting this job?

2. How did Iphigenia finally escape from the Taurians? *(She was rescued by her brother, Orestes.)*

3. Describe a time when a sibling or friend helped you "escape" from a task you detested.

19. The Royal House of Thebes

Synopsis: (a) **Cadmus and His Children**—Cadmus, brother of Europa, went to Apollo for help in finding his sister who was carried away by a bull. He fought a dragon, founded the glorious city of Thebes and married Harmonia. Unfortunately, all of their four daughters met with tragedy: Semele, Ino (whose husband went mad and killed their son), Agave (who went mad and killed her own son), and Autonoe (who had to watch her innocent son die a horrible death).

Discussion/Writing Questions

1. What city was founded by Cadmus? *(Thebes)*

2. What happened to all of Cadmus' daughters? *(All met tragic ends; three had children die. Semele bore Zeus' son, Dionysus, but died when she insisted on seeing Zeus in his glory.)*

3. Do you think the story of Cadmus and his children "speaks to" the incidents of infanticide that have appeared in the news lately? Write a short essay telling how a recent case resembles the myth.

Synopsis: (b) **Oedipus**—Oedipus was the descendent of Cadmus, who unknowingly killed his own father, King Laius, and married his mother. After solving the riddle of the sphinx, he became King of Thebes and ruled for many years. A plague came and Apollo declared that relief would come when King Laius' murder was avenged. Oedipus finally realized the awful truth that he was that murderer and blinded himself. His wife/mother, Jocasta, killed herself in shame.

Discussion/Writing Questions

1. Why did Oedipus kill his father? *(When a man with three attendants on the highway tried to force him off the road, he killed all three, not knowing that one—King Laius—was his father.)*

2. How did Oedipus become King of Thebes and unknowingly marry his own mother? *(When he saved the Thebans by answering the riddle of the sphinx, they made him their king and he married the dead king's wife, Jocasta.)*

3. How did Oedipus finally discover the awful truth about his parents? *(A plague struck Thebes and Apollo declared that it would end only when King Laius' murderer was punished; Oedipus sent for the seer, Tiresias, who told him the truth.)*

4. Why did Oedipus blind himself? *(He was horrified by the realization that he had murdered his father and married his mother, so he sought refuge in blindness.)*

5. What happened to Jocasta? *(She killed herself.)*

6. Was Oedipus a hapless victim or did he bring this terrible series of tragedies on himself?

7. Suppose you are a newspaper editor. A decision has not yet been reached as to what should become of Oedipus, who has turned out to be the murderer of King Laius. Write an editorial that summarizes the case and gives your opinion of what should be done with Oedipus.

Synopsis: (c) **Antigone**—Oedipus' daughter, Antigone, defied her uncle Creon's command that the body of her brother, Polyneices, should not receive proper burial. Her sister tried to accept some of the blame for burying the body, but only Antigone was killed.

Discussion/Writing Questions

1. How did Antigone defy her uncle? Why? With what result? *(She buried her brother because she felt it was her sacred duty. Her uncle had her put to death.)*

2. Why was it so important to Creon that Polyneices be denied a proper burial? *(Polyneices had attacked the city in an attempt to overthrow Creon.)*

3. Why was Antigone killed but not her sister? *(Antigone made it clear that she had gotten no help from her sister.)*

4. Do you think you can understand someone like Antigone who remains loyal despite the near-certain risk of death? Have you read about any "Antigones" in recent news?

5. You are Antigone's sister, Ismene, thinking about your sister months after her death. Three memories float to the surface of your mind—one, when you were little girls; another, the day she asked you to help bury your brother; another, when she was sentenced to die. Describe the memories in prose or poetry form.

Synopsis: (d) **The Seven Against Thebes**—Six other chieftains had helped Polyneices attack the seven gates of Thebes and only one, Adrustus, survived. The Athenians marched against Thebes when Creon would not allow the dead to be claimed. Finally the bodies were properly burned on pyres, but the sons of the dead vowed vengeance and marched on Thebes ten years later, leveling it to the ground.

Discussion/Writing Questions

1. Who were the Seven against Thebes? What happened to them? *(These were seven chieftains who attacked the gates of Thebes; six were killed.)*

2. How did the sons take revenge? *(Ten years later, they leveled Thebes.)* Do you think children should seek revenge for wrongs heaped upon their parents? Can you think of present-day cases like this?

3. Find a newspaper summary about a revenge killing. Summarize the story in a well-written paragraph.

20. The Royal House of Athens

Synopsis: (a) **Cecrops**—Cecrops was the first king of Attica, great-grandfather of Theseus, who decided—after Athena gave the gift of an olive tree—that Athens was hers.

Discussion/Writing Questions
1. How did Athena get to preside over Athens? *(She grew an olive tree—the most prized tree—on the Acropolis, so Cecrops decided that Athens should be hers as a reward.)*

2. What has the olive branch come to symbolize? *(peace)*

3. Describe a time when you "offered someone an olive branch."

Synopsis: (b) **Procne and Philomela**—These are two sisters with a tragic story. Procne's husband Tereus fell in love with her sister Philomela, told Philomela that Procne had died, forced her into a pretended marriage, then cut out her tongue when she realized the truth. Philomela wove the story into a tapestry, which was carried to Procne. Enraged, Procne killed the son who reminded her of her husband and served the boy, boiled up, to his father for dinner. The gods turned all three into birds: Procne became a nightingale, Philomela became a swallow, and Tereus became a hawk.

Discussion/Writing Questions
1. What does this myth tell us about where the nightingale, swallow, and hawk came from? *(Tereus fell in love with his sister-in-law and tricked her into a false marriage; the gods ultimately turned all three into birds.)*

2. Do you think Procne should be punished for killing her son? Was this a case of "malice aforesight"? Could she plead insanity? Was her motivation similar to Medea's? *(No; Medea killed her children with the intention of protecting them.)*

3. Do you think Tereus' punishment fit his crime? *(He unknowingly ate his son, then was turned into an ugly bird.)* What alternate punishment might you suggest to Procne?

4. What would a modern-day soap opera version of this story be like? Write a short script.

Synopsis: (c) **Procris and Cephalus**—Procris, the unfortunate niece of Procne and Philomela, married Cephalus, who was carried off by Aurora, Goddess of the Dawn, who had fallen in love with him. She finally released him, but he doubted that Procris had been faithful. They were finally reconciled, but one day Cephalus accidentally killed Procris while they were out hunting.

Discussion/Writing Questions

1. Why did Aurora carry off Cephalus? *(She was in love with him.)* Was the impact on him any different from what usually happened when gods fell in love with mortal women and ran off with them? *(He remained faithful to his wife.)*

2. Why did Cephalus doubt that Procris had been faithful to him? *(Aurora told him to test his wife, so he disguised himself and although she refused repeated attempts at seduction, she hesitated once.)* In real life, or other stories, does this "planting the seed of doubt" in a lover's mind happen very often?

3. How did Procris die? *(Cephalus accidentally killed her when he saw something move in the thicket while he was hunting with a never-fail javelin she had given him.)* In some versions of the story, she was killed while jealously spying on him from a bush. Which version do you prefer?

4. What is the "aurora borealis"? *("Northern lights"; a radiant emission that appears in the sky as bands of light, resulting from particles guided along the earth's magnetic bands)* What is the "aurora"? *(dawn)*

5. Describe a time when someone "planted the seed of doubt" in your mind. Write a dialogue showing this incident, real or imagined.

Synopsis: (d) **Orithyia and Boreas**—Boreas the North Wind fell in love with Orithyia, a sister of Procris, and carried her off while she was playing on a river bank.

Discussion/Writing Questions

1. How did Boreas treat Orithyia and why? *(He carried her off because he was in love with her.)*

2. What does "boreal" mean? *(pertaining to the North Wind or simply to the North)*

3. Orithyia has filed a lawsuit against Boreas. Write down the statement of the charges you, attorney for Orithyia, are filing.

Synopsis: (e) **Creusa and Ion**—Creusa, another sister of Procris, was abducted by Apollo. She had a child by him, and left the infant to die in a cave. Eventually she married and she and her husband went to Delphi to ask for a child. There she met a young priest, Ion—her son, whom Apollo had rescued from the cave.

Discussion/Writing Questions

1. Why did Creusa abandon her child? *(She was afraid she would be killed if she confessed to having a child with a god.)*

2. How was Creusa reconciled with her son, years later? *(She met him at Delphi when she and her husband went there to ask for a child.)*

3. Is this a happy ending? How do you suppose Creusa felt about Apollo's late reparation for her suffering? Should she forgive and forget?

21. Midas and Others

Synopsis: (a) **Midas**—King Midas entertained the drunken old Silenus and returned him to Bacchus, who rewarded him by giving him one wish. Midas asked to have everything he touched turn to gold. When his food turned to metal, he realized what a foolish wish this was and got rid of his fatal gift by washing in the river Pactolus.

Discussion/Writing Questions

1. What is the version of King Midas with which most schoolchildren are familiar? *(King Midas realizes the error of his ways when he turns his beloved daughter to gold.)* What is the moral of that story? *("Don't be greedy.")* Is that the same lesson we are to learn from the original myth? *(The original myth stresses "Don't be foolish.")*

2. Was Ovid's King Midas more greedy or foolish? *(Most will agree that he was more foolish than greedy.)*

3. What would your one wish be?

4. What does it mean to "cut the Gordian knot"? *(act quickly and decisively in a difficult situation)* How is this term derived from the myth of Midas? *(It was said that whoever could untie the knot of Gordus, Midas' father, would become Lord of Asia; the knot was eventually cut, not untied, by Alexander.)*

5. In a short essay, compare/contrast Midas with a character from another story you know, such as the wife in the fairy tale, "The Fisherman and His Wife."

Synopsis: (b) **Aesculapius**—Apollo loved Coronis, but she loved a mortal, so Apollo had Coronis killed. Apollo raised the child she had born him, Aesculapius, who became a great healer with sacred snakes. In the end, he brought a mortal back to life, incurring the wrath of Zeus who killed the healer.

Discussion/Writing Questions

1. Briefly describe the rise and fall of Aesculapius. *(He was raised by his father, Apollo, and became a famous healer, but was killed by Zeus when he brought a man back to life.)*

2. What does the expression "Don't kill the messenger" mean? How does it apply to this story? *(Don't lash out at the person who brings you bad news, the way Apollo punished his white raven for telling him that Coronis had been unfaithful to him.)*

3. Can you think of any images that associate healing with snakes?

4. In other stories, poems, movies, etc., what happens to those who bring mortals back to life? (e.g., Dr. Frankenstein)

5. Where have you seen images associating medicine and snakes? (e.g., What is the American Medical Association's emblem?)

6. Write the "help wanted" ad to which Aesculapius might respond.

Synopsis: (c) **The Danaids**—These are 50 maidens who killed their husbands, whom they were forced to marry against their wills except for Hypermnestra, who helped her bridegroom flee. The 49 maidens were punished by having to try forever to carry water in leaky jars.

Discussion/Writing Questions

1. How and why were the Danaids punished? *(Because they killed their husbands, they were forced to carry water in leaky jars.)*

2. What is the most frustrating punishment you can think of for the Danaids?

3. Write a limerick about the Danaids.

Synopsis: (d) **Glaucus and Scylla**—Glaucus was a fisherman who was turned into a sea-god. He fell in love with a lovely nymph named Scylla, but she fled in repulsion. He went to Circe the enchantress for help, but she fell in love with him and changed Scylla into a monster rooted to a rock, lashing out in misery at any sailors who came within her reach.

Discussion/Writing Questions

1. Who punished Scylla? How? Why? *(Circe changed the nymph into a monster because Circe was jealous of Glaucus' love for the lovely nymph.)*

2. What do you suppose Glaucus did and felt when he discovered what had happened to Scylla? Should he feel guilty? Should we sympathize with Circe's jealousy or condemn her for her wickedness?

3. Do you think most people who hurt other people deliberately do so out of their own unhappiness?

4. Can you see any connection between Glaucus the sea god and "glaucoma" or "glaucous gull"? *(Glaucoma results in the eye lens becoming a grayish white, is "sea colored"—grayish white.)*

5. Look through Bartlett's Familiar Quotations for a quote that somehow applies to this story about Scylla. Write a paragraph explaining the connection.

Synopsis: (e) **Erysichthon**—When Erysichthon cut down a sacred oak, Ceres punished him by making him starve in the very act of eating. He endlessly sold and resold his daughter, who had the power to escape her owners by assuming different shapes. Eventually he devoured himself.

Discussion/Writing Questions

1. How and why was Erysichthon punished? *(Because he cut down a sacred oak, he was made to go hungry while eating.)*

2. What other stories would you group this one with as evidence of the Greeks' respect for plant life?

3. How was Erysichthon like Phineus and Tantalus? *(Phineus and Tantalus, too, could never satisfy their hunger.)*

4. How was Erysichthon's daughter like Proteus? *(Both could change shapes.)*

5. Did Erysichthon exploit his daughter? *(Yes, he sold her.)* Find a recent news story (or cartoon, ad, etc.) that shows a parallel relationship between father and daughter.

6. How did Erysichthon finally die? *(He devoured his own flesh.)* What do you suppose was his daughter's reaction?

Synopsis: (f) **Pomona and Vertumnus**—Pomona was a nymph who loved the orchards, but had no interest in suitors. Vertumnus disguised himself as an old woman, who told her she should accept Vertumnus. When he dropped his disguise, she yielded to him.

Discussion/Writing Questions

1. Why did Pomona change her mind about Vertumnus? *(She was convinced that she should accept him by the arguments he gave while disguised as an old woman.)*

2. How would you update the idea of Pomona and Vertumnus for a skit set in a typical middle or high school?

3. Do you think a married couple who work together are more or less inclined to stay together?

4. Find out more about Pomona, California, and decide if it is well-named. Where else would you find a place named Pomona? *(largest of the Orkney Islands)* What does "pomme" mean in French? *(apple)* What is "pomiculture"? *(the growing of fruit)* What is pomology? *(science of fruit growing)* What is Pomona glass? *(American art glass stained pale amber on one side and etched on the other)*

5. What do you suppose Pomona and Vertumnus would say to one another if they decided to write their own wedding vows? Write the vows.

22. Brief Myths

Below is an alphabetical listing summarizing the Brief Myths.

Amalthea	A goat with a Horn of Plenty
Amazons	A nation of women-warriors
Amymone	A Danaid pursued by a satyr, saved by Poseidon
Antiope	Princess whose sons killed the ruling couple, Lycus and Dirce, for mistreating their mother
Arachne	Skilled weaver turned into a spider by Minerva
Arion	Dolphins rescued this master of the lyre from the sea

Aristaeus	Beekeeper who seized Proteus and held him as he shape-shifted before revealing how to keep his bees well
Aurora and Tithonus	Goddess of the Dawn and her husband, who was made immortal by Zeus; When aged, Tithonus prayed for death
Biton and Cleobis	Sons of a priestess who died after drawing their mother on a cart through the heat to see a statue
Callisto	Jealous Hera turned her into a bear and Zeus put her in the sky. She became The Great Bear, next to her son, the Lesser Bear
Chiron	The only immortal Centaur, he was accidentally wounded by Hercules and allowed by Zeus to die
Clytie	Maiden in love with the Sun-god, turned into a sunflower
Dryope	Turned into a tree when she plucked a flower from a lotus tree
Epimenides	Boy who searched for a lost sheep and slept for 57 years
Ericthonius	Half-man, half serpent, he became King of Athens
Hero and Leander	Every night Leander swam to the priestess, Hero, until he drowned
Hyades	Rainy stars, daughters of Atlas
Ibycus and the Cranes	A flock of cranes avenged the death of this poet, attacked by robbers
Leto	The island of Delos, unlike other places, welcomed Leto when it was time for her to deliver her children by Zeus; a glorious temple rose up there
Linus	He was a lovely young boy—deserted by his mother, torn to pieces by dogs—who died before he could really live
Marpessa	Apollo fell in love with her, but she chose the mortal, Idas
Marsyas	A flute-playing satyr who dared challenge Apollo to a contest
Melampus	Famous soothsayer whose snakes gave him the gift of understanding the language of animals
Merope	She and her son killed Polyphontes, the man who had killed her first husband and taken her as his wife
Myrmidons	Men created from ants, followers of Achilles
Nisus and Scylla	Scylla fell in love with Minos and betrayed her father by cutting his purple lock of hair
Orion	A great hunter, he was blinded for getting drunk and insulting a maiden; after death he became a constellation
Pleiades	Seven daughters of Atlas, Zeus put them in the heavens as stars to escape Orion's pursuit
Rhoecus	He earned the love of a dryad by saving an oak, but was blinded by her when he injured a bee, her messenger

Salmoneus	He was killed by Zeus for daring to impersonate the god
Sisyphus	Zeus punished him (for revealing that Zeus had abducted a girl) by having him try forever to roll a rock uphill in Hades
Tyro	She abandoned her sons by Poseidon, Neleus and Pelias (who sent Jason after the Golden Fleece)

Writing Questions

1. Write an essay comparing and contrasting two of these figures.

2. Write your opinion of the actions taken by two of these figures.

Bibliography for Teachers

Internet Sites

1. American Classical League, Miami University, Oxford OH 45056-1694

   (Or click on this website: **http://www.umich.edu/~acleague**)

   Here you will find membership information, including information for students interested in joining the National Junior Classical League, a teaching materials and resources center, information on the National Mythology Exam for elementary and middle school students, and links to teaching tools.

2. There are several very good mythology Internet sites on the Web. You might start with the Library of Congress Resources for Classicists, which offers many good links:
   http://lcweb.loc.gov/global/classics

3. Encyclopedia Mythica offers hundreds of definitions of Greek gods and heroes as well as those from other mythologies:
   http://www.pantheon.org/mythica/

4. At the Perseus site, you will find many on-line definitions and pictures, links to related sites, course syllabi—including outlines for several mythology courses—and most important, a description of PERSEUS, a multimedia computer program developed at Yale and used by hundreds of high school and college teachers. It has not only complete works but the largest photographic database of ancient Greece including hundreds of mythological illustrations. This program has received rave reviews from the *New York Times* and many others. Access it at:
   http://www.perseus.tufts.edu/

5. Mythology in Western Art—a site that offers images of the main Greek gods:
   http://www-lib.haifa.ac.il/www/art/MYTHOLOGY-WESTART.HTML

6. The Wesleyan Classics Page offers resources for classical studies on the web:
   http://www.wesleyan.edu/classics/resource.html

7. Many images from ancient sources and later representations in art:
   http://web.UVic.CA/athena/bowman/myth/gods.html

8. Some contemporary art images reflecting mythological themes:
   http://www.parnasse.com/erlist.htm

9. Internet Classics Archive: **http://classics.mit.edu/**

Other Materials

10. *Mythology and You: Classical Mythology and Its Relevance to Today's World*, Donna Rosenberg & Sorelle Baker, National Textbook Co., 1984.

11. To order the six-videotape set, "Joseph Campbell and the Power of Myth," call 1.800.645.4727 or see this PBS website:
    http://www2.pbs.org/store-cgi/store/yljbU5quOH?item=A1216-WWV2

    (In a series of conversations with Bill Moyers, Campbell explains how mythology defines and guides our lives and culture.)

Writing Activities

Essay Exam/Paper Topics

1. Compare and contrast one of the following groups or pairs:

   Cronus and Zeus; Daedalus and Phaethon; Atalanta and Artemis; Perseus, Hercules, Odysseus, and Jason; Chiron, Medusa, Minotaur, Polyphemus, and Scylla/Charybdis; two of the love stories; one of your real-life heroes with one of the Greek heroes

2. Discuss women in Greek mythology. Using specific examples of goddesses and mortals, discuss what the myths show about the conception of women in Greek society. Include references to women's duties to parents, husbands, children, the dead and what various interactions between women and men, women and gods say to you about how women were viewed.

3. What do the various myths tell you about the Greeks' view of death?

4. Discuss several myths which focus on the conflict between Man and Nature.

5. Compare a Greek myth or mythical figure with a similar one from another culture. For example, how does Ares compare with Ogoun, the Haitian god of war? How does the Native American hero Daldal compare with the Greek hero, Hercules? (The Encyclopedia Mythica on the Web contains a lot of information about Norse, Persian, Native American, Chinese, Haitian and other mythologies.)

6. Take a recent current event and discuss how it parallels what happens in one of the Greek myths.

7. Choose a piece of artwork (painting, sculpture, vase, etc.) based on a Greek myth, that particularly strikes you. Discuss the story as treated by the artist. Show that you have thought about what the myth means and how the artist has captured the essence of that myth.

   An excellent resource for this topic is: *Myths of the Greeks and Romans* by Michael Grant with 64 pages of illustrations; Penguin Group, 1995.

8. Analyze mythological aspects of an episode from one of two TV series—"Hercules: The Legendary Journeys" (**http://www.mca.com/tv/hercules**) *or* "Star Trek: The Next Generation" (**http://www.ugcs.caltech.edu/st-tng/episodes/202.html**).

   Ideally, you should analyze an episode you have seen, but you can find synopses at the above websites. Ask yourself: What characters and themes has the episode drawn from mythology? Look for incidents where a name is borrowed gratuitously, e.g., "Nausicaans" to describe a group of countrymen who cheat at the gaming table in an episode of "Star Trek"—and who apparently have no connection with the mythical Nausicaa who helped Odysseus, or Typhon, an uncharted expanse of space apparently named by "Star Trek" script writers after the mythical Typhon.

9. Explain which Greek god or hero you would most like to be and why.

10. Choose your favorite monster from Greek myth and retell his/her story from his or her point of view.

11. Write the conversation that Cronus has with his father and mother and some of the Titans shortly after Zeus has dethroned him.

12. Write the conversation that Persephone has with her mother when they are first reunited at Demeter's temple.

13. Describe a scene where two or more mythological figures meet in Hades, such as Semele and Pentheus.

14. Suppose that some of the women Odysseus met on his ten-year journey (e.g., Calypso, Circe, Nausicaa, the Sirens) visit with Penelope after Odysseus' death. Write the conversation that they have over tea.

15. Write a summary, or even a short screenplay, that incorporates a story, character, or theme from Greek myth into an episode of "Star Trek" or "Hercules, The Legendary Journeys."

16. Make a gift list for a mythological figure.

17. Describe what you would find in a particular mythological figure's pockets.

18. Describe a mythological figure's favorite place.

19. Write a letter of advice to a god or goddess or hero.

20. Write a song about a figure from mythology.

21. Assume the persona of one of the gods or goddesses or humans from mythology and write a "personals" ad.

22. There are many killings in these stories. Write a "wanted" poster (for example, for the murderer of Laius).

23. Create a newspaper based on some of the gods, goddesses, heroes, and places that figure in Greek myth.

24. Try to create clues for a word puzzle that transforms one mythological figure into another (e.g., Zeus turns into bull, men turn into pigs, a maiden turns into a spider). Each clue should elicit a word that is one letter different from the word in the previous step.

At the right is a sample that refers to the transformation of Daphne into a laurel tree. (Students should provide the thirteen clues.)

GIRL
GIRD
GIRT
DIRT
DIME
DIMS
DIES
TIES
TIER
BIER
BRER
BREE
TREE

25. Write in Question/Answer form the interview you hold with a mythological figure

26. Make a list of famous figures from mythology, add clues, and use a piece of software to generate a crossword puzzle.

27. Pretend that you are a comedian. Write a monologue in which you lampoon a political figure by comparing him to a mythological one, e.g., comparing a politician-womanizer to Zeus.

28. Choose any story or figure from mythology you wish—mortal, god, creature, etc. Find out all that you can about how that figure has been portrayed by various authors, artists, sculptors, musicians, etc. Keep a log of your on-line activity. (Two sites that are excellent starting points are PERSEUS and the Smithsonian Institute On-Line.) Keep a record of all sources you consult, including written sources, electronic ones, experts, art books, etc. Summarize your findings in the form of an illustrated essay complete with photographs of such things as vases, paintings, etc., either taken off the Internet, or photocopied from books. Sample topics:

- How Zeus has been portrayed by various artists
- Parallel myths of other cultures (such as Clytemnestra's story and the Norse tale of Signy; or Cupid and Psyche and the Norse folktale, "East of the Sun and West of the Moon")
- Comparison of the creation story and the characteristics of gods and goddesses within Greek and Norse mythology
- The impact of the tale of Demeter and Persephone on contemporary literature
- Helen as seen by Euripides, Aeschylus, Sappho and other ancient writers
- A comparison between various contemporary writers' versions of the same story (e.g., the Daedalus myth as revisited by Ian Serraillier, Gerald McDermott, and Penelope Farmer). These writers also tell different versions of various myths: Olivia Coolidge, Charles Kingsley, and Padraic Colum.

29. Compare the Greek creation story with stories from other cultures. A good source: Virginia Hamilton's *In the Beginning: Creation Stories from Around the World.*

30. Write your own myth, using the Greek myths you have read as models. As you write, consider that Greek myths often

> —account for how the world and humans originated
> —explain how natural phenomena (e.g., seasons, plants, animals) came to be
> —address universal human experience (e.g., love, death)
> —include animals, deities, and/or humans
> —take place in an earlier world (or another world)
> —reveal something about Greek values, often by showing gods punishing mortals for wrong-doing
> —tell us something about Greek religious belief
> —say something about how the roles of men and women are viewed
> —address such themes as fate, obedience, piety, death, war, friendship, happiness, loyalty

31. As a group research project, divide the class into small groups, each responsible for giving part of a "chart talk" about the Greek and Roman gods and goddesses. A scribe from each group fills in the group's contribution to the chart. A spokesperson for the group explains what the group learned and shares an illustration and story about the god/goddess from a particular illustrated text (e.g., D'Aulaire's *Book of Greek Myths* or Leonard Everett Fisher's *The Olympians*).

Name	Accomplishments	Powers	Group's choice of text
(Greek and Roman)			(title, author, page)

32. Write a sequel to one of the Greek myths or an adaptation. For example, you might write another adventure for Odysseus, tell the story of an Odysseus-like figure in the 21st century, write a "Star Trek" episode about an Odysseus-like figure, etc.

Listening/Speaking/Drama

1. Act out a trial for a figure in Greek myth (e.g., Persephone, Prometheus, Oedipus, Arachne, Daedalus, Echo, Ixion, Bellerophon, Paris, Phineus).

2. Stage a debate about (a) one of the statements listed in the Anticipation Guide (page 5), or (b) whether or not a particular figure from mythology did the right thing, e.g., "Should Penelope have remained faithful?"

3. Act out an episode from a popular TV talk show in which several figures from mythology appear, e.g., "women who have killed their husbands" or "pathological liars."

4. Choose your favorite myth and record it on audiotape for a classroom listening library.

5. Act out your favorite myth (or a situation in which a particular character might have found himself, but didn't).

6. Students play "20 Questions." One person leaves the group while the others choose a mythological figure. The person who is "it" returns and asks at most 20 questions with a Yes/No answer, in an attempt to guess whom the group has chosen.

7. Have students act out their favorite myth in pantomime while others try to guess which story is being enacted.

Art/Music

1. Create a *papier-mâché* mask and/or costume depicting one of the monsters or creatures (e.g., Typhon, Pegasus, Cyclops) for a "come as your favorite mythological creature" party. Serve "ambrosia."

2. Capture your favorite myth on videotape, or in a painting, sculpture, or song.

3. Help your teacher make slides or transparencies of mythological illustrations (e.g., those found in Michael Grant's *Myths of the Greeks and Romans*). (Teachers could use these in creating a slide identification portion of the final exam students take on their mythology unit.)

4. Create a poster showing the gods and goddesses of Mt. Olympus, with a brief description of each.

5. Create a travel poster to entice visitors to one of the spots that figures in a particular myth, such as the Labyrinth.

6. Design a board game or card game based on mythology.

7. Design some stationery featuring a figure from mythology using computer clip art or inking stamps you make yourself using cut potatoes.

Language Study

1. Create an illustrated booklet of various words and phrases from Greek mythology that have entered the English language.

2. Create a list of similes and metaphors with mythological references (e.g., "Cleaning my room is like tidying up the Augean stables...").

Research

1. Find out about the origins of the Olympic games.

2. On maps of ancient Greece, locate sites mentioned in various myths, e.g., Mt. Olympus in Thessaly—northeastern Greece; the Ionian sea along which Io ran; Thebes—home of Hercules; the island of Cythera—near which Aphrodite was born; Corinth—where Pegasus' stable was located, etc.

3. Certain authors are known for studding their stories with allusions. Comb one of these for references to classical mythology, using the Internet. Write a 2-3 page report describing the allusions you found and how they were used, in the context of the story. (You might want to consult an on-line version of a Shakespearean play or a Thomas Hardy novel, for example, using the "Search" command to look for particular mythical figures.)

4. On a United States map, find some places that take their names from mythology, e.g., Mt. Olympus in Washington State; Jupiter, Florida; Athens, Ohio; Atlanta, Georgia.

Current Events

1. Make a collection of headlines, ads, cartoons, etc. that contain references to Greek mythology.

2. Make a bulletin board display showing various recent news events and labeling each with an explanation of how it ties in with a particular myth.

Assessment for *Mythology*

Assessment is an ongoing process. The following twelve items can be completed during the novel study. Once finished, the student and teacher will check the work. Points may be added to indicate the level of understanding.

Name _____ Date _____

Student   **Teacher**

_____ _____   1.   As you read the myths, keep a Response Log in which you jot down your reactions and questions.

_____ _____   2.   Write your own myth that explains the origin of a geographical feature in your area.

_____ _____   3.   Write an interior monologue that reveals the thoughts of a Greek god, goddess, or human as (s)he faces a problem.

_____ _____   4.   Create a board game that incorporates the key events of a favorite myth. Include directions for playing.

_____ _____   5.   Summarize one of your favorite myths as a five-frame cartoon strip.

_____ _____   6.   Work on a group mural that shows a journey taken by a Greek hero.

_____ _____   7.   Act out a trial for a figure from Greek mythology such as Persephone or Arachne.

_____ _____   8.   Act out a TV talk show on which three mythological figures make appearances.

_____ _____   9.   Give your impressions of a favorite myth in the form of a collage, drawing, or song.

_____ _____   10. Write an essay using one of the topics on pages 34-37 of this guide.

_____ _____   11. Alternative activity of your choice...

_____ _____   12. Write a self-evaluation of your portfolio, explaining the strengths and weaknesses of various pieces and assigning yourself an overall grade.

Note: For quizzes, tests, a study guide, and activity sheets focusing on critical thinking skills, vocabulary study, literary analysis, and writing skills, see the **Novel Units® Student Packet** for *Mythology*.